ANIMAL SURVIVAL

MIGRATING TO SURVIVE

BY CLARA MacCARALD

CONTENT CONSULTANT
CHRISTOPHER M. SWAN, PhD
PROFESSOR
DEPT. OF GEOGRAPHY & ENVIRONMENTAL SYSTEMS
UNIVERSITY OF MARYLAND

Kids Core

An Imprint of Abdo Publishing
abdobooks.com

abdobooks.com

Published by Abdo Publishing, a division of ABDO, PO Box 398166, Minneapolis, Minnesota 55439. Copyright © 2023 by Abdo Consulting Group, Inc. International copyrights reserved in all countries. No part of this book may be reproduced in any form without written permission from the publisher. Kids Core™ is a trademark and logo of Abdo Publishing.

Printed in the United States of America, North Mankato, Minnesota.
052022
092022

Cover Photo: Petr Simon/Shutterstock Images
Interior Photos: Mark Newman/The Image Bank/Getty Images, 4–5; Jo Crebbin/Shutterstock Images, 6; Shutterstock Images, 8, 20, 22–23, 24, 28 (top); iStockphoto, 10–11, 14, 29 (top); Tony Campbell/Shutterstock Images, 12; Robert McGillivray/Shutterstock Images, 16–17; Ingo Arndt/Nature Picture Library/Alamy, 19, 29 (bottom); E. Hughes/iStockphoto, 26, 28 (bottom)

Editor: Ann Schwab
Series Designer: Katharine Hale

Library of Congress Control Number: 2021951729

Publisher's Cataloging-in-Publication Data

Names: MacCarald, Clara, author.
Title: Migrating to survive / by Clara MacCarald
Description: Minneapolis, Minnesota : Abdo Publishing, 2023 | Series: Animal survival | Includes online resources and index.
Identifiers: ISBN 9781532198533 (lib. bdg.) | ISBN 9781644947708 (pbk.) | ISBN 9781098272180 (ebook)
Subjects: LCSH: Animal defenses--Juvenile literature. | Defense measures--Juvenile literature. | Adaptation (Physiology)--Juvenile literature. | Animal behavior--Juvenile literature.
Classification: DDC 591.57--dc23

CONTENTS

Sandhill cranes stop by the Platte River in Nebraska on their spring migration north to Canada.

CHAPTER 1

A MIGRATION STOPOVER

The sun has not yet risen in Nebraska. The wide, shallow Platte River is silent. A sandhill crane makes a call. More cranes answer it. The river comes to life with sound. As the sun rises, it reveals a giant flock of sandhill cranes.

At the end of their migration journey, the cranes will nest and raise their young. This mother is watching over her two-day-old chicks.

Hundreds of thousands of sandhill cranes stop at the Platte River every spring. They are migrating north. Migration is a regular journey from one place to another, often to find food or to have young. At the end of migration, a pair of cranes will nest. Together they will raise chicks before returning south.

Birds of North America

Billions of North American birds migrate north every spring and south every fall. About 350 **species** travel as far away as Central and South America. The huge numbers of birds can even be seen on weather radar.

More than 1.5 million wildebeests migrate each year through Tanzania and Kenya as they follow the seasonal rains to find food. It is one of the largest animal migrations in the world.

Journeying to Survive

Animals migrate for many different reasons.

Some species leave areas for the winter to

find warmer weather. They might go where food is more plentiful. Other animals travel to avoid predators or go elsewhere to **mate** or have young. They may follow ocean currents or use the position of the sun to find their way. Migration helps each of these species survive.

Explore Online

Visit the website below. What new information did you learn about migration that wasn't in Chapter One?

How and Why Animals Migrate

abdocorelibrary.com/migrating-to -survive

A salmon jumps
upstream during its river
migration journey.

CHAPTER 2

WATER VOYAGES

Many animals make their journeys through water. Pacific salmon are found in the northern Pacific waters of the United States and Canada. Some species may cover up to 2,500 miles (4,000 km) during migration.

Salmon are hunted by many predators, including bald eagles, during migration.

Salmon are born in freshwater lakes and rivers. They later migrate to the ocean and spend their adult lives there. When it is time for them to **spawn**, the fish return to the same location in which they were born. The journey both ways is long and hard. They face danger from predators. There is little food available. Those that arrive home die soon after spawning. After their eggs hatch, the cycle starts over again.

A Whale's Tale

Humpback whales spend the summer in cool waters, near polar regions. There, plenty of food is available. When the weather turns cold, it's time to migrate.

Using Magnetic Fields to Steer

Earth creates a huge **magnetic field**. It has lines that run from the North Pole to the South Pole. Many animals can sense this field. Fish, birds, and other animals use it to find their way while migrating.

Humpback whales migrate to tropical waters to have young.

Some humpback whales migrate up to 5,000 miles (8,000 km). They spend the winter in **tropical** waters. There, the whales mate and have their calves. The young calves would not survive in the colder climates. Adult whales have a layer of fat called blubber to protect them from the cold. But newborn calves don't have this.

Marine biologist Dr. Helen Scales explains how Pacific salmon find their way home:

> Salmon remember the magnetic fields they encountered when they first entered the sea as youngsters and navigate their way back to the exact same stream where they were born.

Source: Helen Scales. "How Do Salmon Find Their Way Home?" *Science Focus*, n.d., sciencefocus.com. Accessed 27 Jan. 2022.

What's the Big Idea?

Read this quote carefully. What is its main idea? Explain how the main idea is supported by details.

Emperor penguins migrate inland to mate and raise their chicks.

CHAPTER 3

JOURNEYS OVER LAND

Animals migrate over land on every continent. Emperor penguins live in Antarctica. In March, they migrate inland from the sea. They travel 100 miles (161 km). Each female lays an egg and then returns to the sea to find food.

Each male penguin stays behind to care for his partner's egg. By August, the chicks have hatched and the females have returned. They take care of the chicks while the males journey to the sea to feed. The cycle continues until the chicks are old enough to travel to the sea with their parents.

Crab Crossings

When Christmas Island red crabs migrate, they must cross roads. Cars may run over them. To protect the crabs, some roads are closed to drivers. People have also built crab crossings. Some crossings are tunnels under the road. The crabs can also climb up and down a crab bridge.

In the fall, millions of Christmas Island red crabs migrate to the ocean to mate.

Crabs on the Move

Christmas Island red crabs live only on the Australian island that gives them their name. Adult crabs live in the rain forests. Every fall, millions of the crabs migrate together to the ocean. Once they reach the shore, the males dig burrows. Males and females then mate. The females settle into the burrows while the males return home.

Caribou travel through Canada's Northwest Territories during their fall migration.

After two weeks, the mothers gather at the shore in huge mobs. Together they release all their eggs into the water. After a month, baby crabs start migrating to the rain forests.

Caribou Journeys

Caribou are wild reindeer native to North America. Some caribou populations have the longest land migrations of any animal. Caribou in northwest Alaska migrate up to 2,737 miles (4,405 km) in a year.

In the summer, caribou live on treeless plains near the Arctic. They feast on grass and other low plants. Female caribou give birth in late spring. There are few predators in this area, so the calves are protected. In the fall, the weather gets colder and snow begins to cover the ground, so less food is available. The herd moves south. Caribou spend the winter in forests eating **lichens**.

Further Evidence

Look at the website below. Does it give any new evidence to support Chapter Three?

What Is an Emperor Penguin?

abdocorelibrary.com/migrating-to -survive

A flock of arctic terns takes flight during the birds' migration journey.

CHAPTER 4

AIR FLIGHTS

Lots of creatures fly to migrate. Arctic terns are small seabirds. They hold the record for the longest migration of any animal. Scientists found one bird that had flown almost 60,000 miles (97,000 km) in a year.

Arctic Tern Migration

Nesting Grounds
Greenland, Iceland
June 1–August 1

September 1

October 1

May 1

November 1

November 1

Winter Grounds
Antarctica
December 1–April 1

This map shows where arctic terns live at different times of the year. The arrows show their migration paths.

Arctic terns nest in the Arctic. But when winter arrives, the birds migrate to the southern polar region. They seek longer days of sunlight.

This helps them hunt for food. They fly by the coasts of every continent. Being small and light helps terns ride the wind.

Butterfly Trek

Many monarch butterflies spend the winter in Mexico and California. Monarchs can't survive the cold, so they roost together to stay warm. Tens of thousands can cover a single tree.

Monarchs That Stay Put

Not all monarchs need to migrate. In parts of Florida, the weather stays warm enough for the butterflies all year long. Milkweed, the plant they eat, grows all winter too. So monarchs in those areas don't have to travel.

Monarch butterflies cluster together on a tree during their migration journey to California.

In the spring, the monarchs begin flying north. They sometimes travel almost 1,865 miles (3,000 km). Monarchs in western North America have large wings and small bodies. Scientists believe this helps them fly long distances.

Migration is a valuable tool for animals. It protects them from predators. It helps them avoid bad weather. It also helps them obtain food. Migration is a skill they use to survive.

Scientist Richard Bevan studies arctic tern migration. He said:

> It's really quite humbling to see these tiny birds return when you consider the huge distances they've had to travel and how they've battled to survive.

Source: "Record-Breaking Bird Migration Revealed in New Research." *Newcastle University*, 7 June 2016, ncl.ac.uk. Accessed 15 Dec. 2021.

Point of View

What is the author's point of view on this topic? What is your point of view? Write a short essay about how they are similar and different.

SURVIVAL FACTS

Many animals migrate to find food.

Some animals migrate to avoid certain weather conditions.

Animals may migrate to a place where they can lay eggs, give birth, or raise young.

Some animals migrate to a place for mating.

ROAD CLOSED
RED CRAB MIGRATION
NO ENTRY BY VEHICLES
BEYOND THIS POINT

Glossary

lichens
organisms composed of a fungus in union with algae or bacteria

magnetic field
the place in space in which electrical charges are observed

mate
to come together to have young

spawn
in fish, to release many small eggs in water

species
groups of similar living things that can have young together

tropical
having to do with the hot areas around the imaginary horizontal line that divides Earth into a north and south region

Online Resources

To learn more about migrating to survive, visit our free resource websites below.

Visit **abdocorelibrary.com** or scan this QR code for free Common Core resources for teachers and students, including vetted activities, multimedia, and booklinks, for deeper subject comprehension.

Visit **abdobooklinks.com** or scan this QR code for free additional online weblinks for further learning. These links are routinely monitored and updated to provide the most current information available.

Learn More

Huddleston, Emma. *How Birds Fly.* Abdo, 2021.

Murray, Julie. *Humpback Whales.* Abdo, 2020.

Thomas, Rachael L. *Animal Migrator Match-Up.* Abdo, 2020.

Index

About the Author

Clara MacCarald is a freelance writer with a master's degree in ecology and natural resources. She lives with her family in an off-grid house nestled in the forests of central New York. When not parenting her daughter, she spends her time writing nonfiction books for kids.